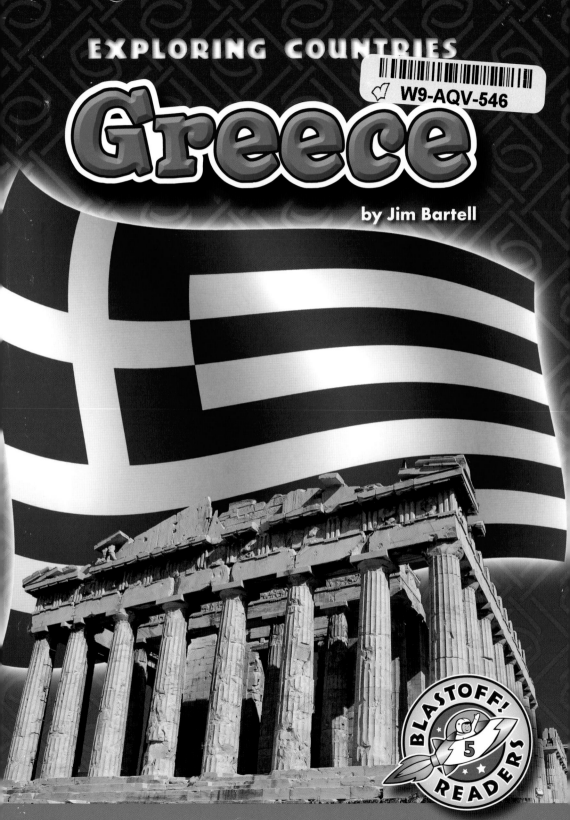

EXPLORING COUNTRIES

Greece

by Jim Bartell

W9-AQV-546

BLASTOFF! READERS 5

BELLWETHER MEDIA • MINNEAPOLIS, MN

Note to Librarians, Teachers, and Parents:

Blastoff! Readers are carefully developed by literacy experts and combine standards-based content with developmentally appropriate text.

Level 1 provides the most support through repetition of high-frequency words, light text, predictable sentence patterns, and strong visual support.

Level 2 offers early readers a bit more challenge through varied simple sentences, increased text load, and less repetition of high-frequency words.

Level 3 advances early-fluent readers toward fluency through increased text and concept load, less reliance on visuals, longer sentences, and more literary language.

Level 4 builds reading stamina by providing more text per page, increased use of punctuation, greater variation in sentence patterns, and increasingly challenging vocabulary.

Level 5 encourages children to move from "learning to read" to "reading to learn" by providing even more text, varied writing styles, and less familiar topics.

Whichever book is right for your reader, Blastoff! Readers are the perfect books to build confidence and encourage a love of reading that will last a lifetime!

This edition first published in 2011 by Bellwether Media, Inc.

No part of this publication may be reproduced in whole or in part without written permission of the publisher. For information regarding permission, write to Bellwether Media, Inc., Attention: Permissions Department, 5357 Penn Avenue South, Minneapolis, MN 55419.

Library of Congress Cataloging-in-Publication Data
Bartell, Jim.
 Greece / by Jim Bartell.
    p. cm. – (Exploring countries) (Blastoff! readers)
Includes bibliographical references and index.
 Summary: "Developed by literacy experts for students in grades three through seven, this book introduces young readers to the geography and culture of Greece"–Provided by publisher.
ISBN 978-1-60014-574-2 (hardcover : alk. paper)
1. Greece–Juvenile literature. I. Title.
DF717.B37 2011
949.5–dc22   2010039126

Printed in the United States of America, North Mankato, MN.

010111   1176

Contents

Bulgaria

Macedonia

Albania

Greece

Aegean Sea

Athens ★

Ionian Sea

Mediterranean Sea

Crete

Did you know?

Greece is often said to be the meeting point of Africa, Asia, and Europe because of its location between the three continents.

Turkey

Greece is a country in southeastern Europe, on the Balkan **Peninsula**. The country's mainland and more than 2,000 islands cover a total of 50,949 square miles (131,957 square kilometers). Albania, Macedonia, Bulgaria, and Turkey border Greece to the north. Part of Turkey lies across the Aegean Sea to the east. To the west, the Ionian Sea separates Greece from Italy. The Mediterranean Sea touches the southern coast of Greece and holds the country's largest island, Crete. Athens, the capital of Greece, is located on the southeastern coast of the mainland.

Mountains and **lowlands** cover most of Greece's landscape. The Pindos Mountains run through northern Greece and end at the Peloponnese peninsula. This peninsula is connected to the mainland by the **Isthmus** of Corinth. The Olympus mountain range is located in the center of Greece.

Many rivers flow down from Greece's mountains and into the lowlands. Wide plains and thick forests fill these flat regions.

Mount Olympus

fun fact

Mount Olympus, the tallest peak in Greece, stands 9,570 feet (2,917 meters) tall. The ancient Greeks believed that their gods lived on this peak.

Did you know?

The Metéora monasteries stand on tall pillars of rock near the Pindos Mountains. Metéora means "suspended in the air" in Greek.

The island of Crete lies in the Mediterranean Sea. It is a long, narrow island that stretches for 162 miles (260 kilometers). At its widest point, it measures only 37 miles (60 kilometers) across. Mountain ranges run the length of the island.

Archaeologists have found **artifacts** on Crete. They believe people lived there over 130,000 years ago. The first known **civilization** on Crete was the Minoan civilization. The Minoans were farmers, fishermen, traders, and artists. They were one of the first civilizations in Europe.

Minoan ruins

dolphin

The landscape of Greece is home to many kinds of wildlife. In northern Greece, bears, deer, and boars roam through forests and on mountains. Farther south, the warmer weather is perfect for porcupines, wild goats, and hares. Pine martens watch the skies for hawks, owls, and other **raptors**.

pine marten

sperm whale

olive tree

! fun fact

Greece has millions of olive trees. The olive tree was sacred to the ancient Greeks. They believed it was a gift from the goddess Athena.

The seas around Greece hold a variety of animals. Dolphins, sharks, and stingrays feed on the many kinds of fish. A few hundred sperm whales swim in the Mediterranean Sea. Their large size keeps them safe from predators. Some live to be 70 years old!

Over 10.5 million people call Greece their home. Nine out of every ten Greek people have **ancestors** who were born in Greece. Many **immigrants** have also come to Greece from neighboring countries. Most of these people come from Albania, Bulgaria, and Romania.

Almost everyone in Greece speaks Greek, the official language of the country. This language has been around for thousands of years and is written in the Greek alphabet. Different regions have their own **dialects**. On the island of Crete, they speak a dialect called Cretan.

Speak Greek!

Greek words can be written in the English alphabet so you can read them out loud!

English	Greek	How to say it
hello	geiá sou	yia su
good-bye	antío	ah-DEE-oh
yes	nai	neh
no	ohi	OH-hi
please	parakaló	pa-ra-ka-LOH
thank you	efcharisto	ef-kha-ri-STOH
friend (male)	filos	FEE-los
friend (female)	fili	FEE-lee

laiki agora

In cities, Greeks live in crowded apartment buildings. They drive cars and ride buses to get around town. Many people buy groceries and other goods at large supermarkets. Most neighborhoods also have *laikes agores*, or "people's markets," where people can buy fresh food.

In the countryside, people live in houses on farms or in small towns. They shop at their local *laiki agora* or at larger stores in the cities. Most people own cars, but many also ride trains from place to place.

Where People Live in Greece

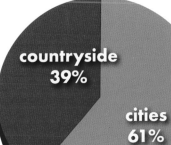

countryside 39%

cities 61%

! fun fact

Large boats called ferries transport people between Greece's many islands.

Greek children must attend school from ages 6 to 15. Primary school lasts for six years. Students learn science, math, Greek, and other subjects. Children go to secondary school for the next three years. After completing those years, students decide if they want to continue with school. Some go to **vocational school** to train for specific jobs. Others continue with secondary school for three more years. Those students can then apply to a university.

fun fact

The largest university in Greece is the Aristotle University of Thessaloniki. Today, over 90,000 students attend the university and study a wide range of subjects.

Where People Work in Greece

manufacturing 23%

services 65%

farming 12%

Did you know?

Greece is the largest producer of extra-virgin olive oil in the world.

Many Greeks in cities have **service jobs**. They work in banks, schools, government offices, and other places. Many people help the millions of **tourists** who visit Greece every year. They have jobs in hotels, restaurants, and museums. Several cities also have factories where workers make clothing, chemicals, and metals.

In the countryside, farmers grow wheat, corn, olives, tomatoes, and other crops. Many raise goats for meat and dairy products, or sheep for wool. In mountain regions, miners dig up iron ore, lead, zinc, and other **minerals**. Along the coasts, fishermen catch fish, lobsters, and other seafood.

Did you know?
Greece has been a part of the International Basketball Federation since 1932.

Greece has a long tradition of sports. It was home to the first **Olympics** almost 3,000 years ago. Today, the most popular sport in the country is soccer. Professionals play the sport in stadiums across Europe. Children play it in their town squares. Basketball and volleyball are two other favorite sports in the country.

Many Greeks enjoy outdoor activities. Hikers, skiers, and mountain climbers take to the slopes. Surfers, sailors, and swimmers spend time in the waters of the surrounding seas.

Did you know?

The gyro might be Greece's most famous food. It includes meat, tomatoes, cucumbers, onions, and feta cheese stuffed into thin pita bread.

The Greeks have cooked with olive oil for thousands of years. Today, it remains the most important ingredient in many Greek dishes. It is commonly used as a dressing on the famous Greek salad. This salad includes lettuce, tomatoes, olives, cucumbers, onions, and feta cheese. Greeks also soak meat in olive oil with salt and pepper. This enhances the meat's flavor as it cooks.

Although some dishes are popular throughout Greece, many are regional. *Souvlaki* is a dish served on a skewer. Along the coasts, it may include fish, shrimp, and other seafood. Farther inland, the skewers often have lamb, pork, or chicken. For dessert, many Greeks enjoy *baklava*, a pastry with layers of nuts and honey.

Greek salad

souvlaki

Ohi Day

Greece has many holidays that mark events in its history. On March 25, Greeks celebrate the day they gained their independence from the **Ottoman Empire**. October 28 is *Ohi* Day. On this day in 1940, Greece's prime minister refused to let Italian and German troops into the country during World War II. His reply was simply *ohi*, or "no."

Most Greeks are Christians and celebrate Christmas, Easter, and other Christian holidays. The Christmas holiday season begins on December 6 with the Feast of St. Nicholas. It ends on January 6 with the Feast of the **Epiphany**. Special honey cookies, or *melomakarona*, are made during the holiday season.

melomakarona

Did you know?
The Greek word *acropolis* means "the highest point of the town."

The acropolis of Athens towers above the rest of the city. For thousands of years, it has been home to palaces and other important buildings. The Parthenon is the most famous building on the acropolis. It was built over 2,000 years ago and dedicated to the Greek goddess Athena, the protector of the people of Athens.

Parthenon

Over the years, it has been used as a church, a **treasury**, and a **mosque**. Today, millions of tourists come to Athens to see the acropolis. The Greek people are trying to restore many of the buildings there. They want to preserve and share the symbols of their country's long history and ancient culture.

Fast Facts About Greece

Greece's Flag

The flag of Greece has nine horizontal stripes, four white and five blue. The stripes represent the nine syllables in the Greek words for "freedom or death." In the upper left corner is a white cross on a blue background, which stands for the Greek Orthodox Church. The flag was officially adopted in 1822.

Official Name: Greece

Area: 50,949 square miles
(131,957 square kilometers);
Greece is the 96th largest
country in the world.

Capital City:	Athens
Important Cities:	Thessaloniki, Pátrai, Iráklion
Population:	10,749,943 (July 2010)
Official Language:	Greek
National Holiday:	Independence Day (March 25)
Religions:	Christian (98%), Other (2%)
Major Industries:	farming, fishing, manufacturing, mining, services, shipping
Natural Resources:	iron ore, oil, zinc, lead, nickel, marble, salt
Manufactured Products:	clothing, food products, metals, chemicals
Farm Products:	olives, olive oil, wheat, corn, sugar beets, tomatoes, potatoes, pork, beef, dairy products
Unit of Money:	euro; the euro is divided into 100 cents.

Glossary

ancestors—relatives who lived long ago

archaeologists—scientists who study the remains of past civilizations

artifacts—items made long ago by humans; artifacts tell people today about people from the past.

civilization—a highly developed, organized society

dialects—unique ways of speaking a language; dialects are often specific to regions of a country.

Epiphany—a Christian holiday that celebrates the three magi visiting Jesus

immigrants—people who leave one country to live in another country

isthmus—a narrow strip of land that lies between two bodies of water; an isthmus connects two larger pieces of land.

lowlands—areas of land that are lower than the surrounding land

minerals—elements found in nature; iron, lead, and nickel are examples of minerals.

mosque—a building that Muslims use for worship

Olympics—international games held every two years; the Olympics alternate between summer sports and winter sports.

Ottoman Empire—a large empire that controlled parts of Europe, Asia, and northern Africa; the Ottoman Empire existed from 1299 to 1923.

peninsula—a section of land that extends out from a larger piece of land and is almost completely surrounded by water

raptors—birds of prey

service jobs—jobs that perform tasks for people or businesses

tourists—people who are visiting a country

treasury—a structure used to store valuables such as gold, silver, and jewels

vocational school—a school that trains students to do specific jobs

To Learn More

AT THE LIBRARY

Bailey, Linda. *Adventures in Ancient Greece.* Toronto, Ont.: Kids Can Press, 2002.

Gay, Kathlyn. *Science in Ancient Greece.* New York, N.Y.: Franklin Watts, 1998.

Sasek, Miroslav. *This is Greece.* New York, N.Y.: Universe Pub., 2009.

ON THE WEB

Learning more about Greece is as easy as 1, 2, 3.

1. Go to www.factsurfer.com.

2. Enter "Greece" into the search box.

3. Click the "Surf" button and you will see a list of related Web sites.

With factsurfer.com, finding more information is just a click away.

Index

The images in this book are reproduced through the courtesy of: Brent Wong, front cover; Maisei Raman, front cover (flag), p. 28; Jon Eppard, pp. 4-5; Alan Novelli / Alamy, pp. 6-7; Imagestate Media Partners Limited – Impact Photos / Alamy, p. 6 (small); Juergen Richter / Photolibrary, p. 8; Kuttig – Travel / Alamy, p. 8 (small); Ian Dagnall / Alamy, p. 9; Frédéric Larrey / Photolibrary, pp. 10-11; Henry Wilson, pp. 11 (top & bottom), 15 (small), 23 (left & right), 29 (bill); Reinhard Dirscherl / Photolibrary, p. 11 (middle); aleksandra lewis / Alamy, p. 12; Frilet Patrick / Photolibrary, p. 14; Travelshots.com / Alamy, p. 15; Peter Horree / Alamy, pp. 16-17; Pete Titmuss / Alamy, p. 18; Paul Cowan, p. 19 (left); colinspics / Alamy, p. 19 (right); EB via Getty Images, p. 20; Look Die Bildagentur der Fotografen GmbH / Alamy, p. 21; Xenia Demetriou - xeniaphotos.com / Alamy, p. 22; Ronald de Heer / Alamy, pp. 24-25; IML Image Group Ltd / Alamy, p. 25 (small); nagelestock.com / Alamy, pp. 26-27; Tomo Jesenicnik, p. 29 (coin).